# FOR CHURCH

**AMY ADAM**
**MIKE HANNICKEL**

EXCLUSIVELY DISTRIBUTED BY

**HAL•LEONARD®**
CORPORATION

7777 W. BLUEMOUND RD. P.O. BOX 13819 MILWAUKEE, WI 53213

**Edition Number: CMP 0868.03**

**Amy Adam, Mike Hannickel**
**TONS OF TUNES for Church**
**Flute / Oboe**

**ISBN 90-431-1973-3**

**CD number: 19.047-3 CMP**

**CD arrangements by James L. Hosay**

# ARRANGERS

**MIKE HANNICKEL** grew up in the Sacramento, California area and attended California State University, Sacramento and the University of Southern California. He has been a music teacher in Rocklin, California since 1973. He also composes and publishes exclusively with Curnow Music Press, with whom he has dozens of pieces of music in print.

**AMY ADAM** was raised in Grand Rapids, Minnesota and attended the University of Minnesota, Duluth graduating with a BM in band education and Flute performance. She has been a music teacher in California since 1992 and currently teaches in Rocklin, California.

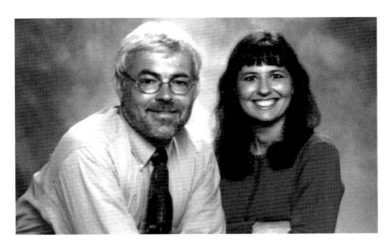

# TONS OF TUNES

**TONS OF TUNES FOR CHURCH** is filled with fun and familiar pieces that musicians love to play. All the songs have been arranged in easy keys for wind instruments. The **professional quality accompaniment CD** can be used for practice and performance. You may also choose to purchase the separately available Piano accompaniment part.

### TO THE MUSIC TEACHER OR CHURCH MUSIC DIRECTOR:
**TONS OF TUNES for CHURCH** is a great way to help get young musicians actively involved in your church music program. Every tune in the book can be performed with the included CD accompaniment or with the separately available Piano/Organ book. All **TONS OF TUNES for CHURCH** books can be used alone or together so a variety of small ensembles can be created. Whether for prelude, offertory, church social, talent show or any other gathering, **TONS OF TUNES for CHURCH** is just what you need. Chord symbols are provided in the Piano accompaniment book for Keyboard, Guitar and combo use.

### TO THE MUSICIAN:
Have **FUN** playing these songs alone or with your family and friends! Even if you have different instruments, you can still play together. Each person needs to get the **TONS OF TUNES FOR CHURCH** book for their instrument.

# FOR CHURCH
## CONTENTS

# TONS OF TUNES FOR CHURCH

**Amy Adam** (ASCAP) and
**Mike Hannickel** (ASCAP)

## 1. ABIDE WITH ME

**TRACK** 3

## 2. NOW THANK WE ALL OUR GOD

**TRACK** 4

# 3. DO, LORD

# 4. BEAUTIFUL SAVIOR

# 5. FOR THE BEAUTY OF THE EARTH

# 6. HOLY, HOLY, HOLY

# 7. JESUS LOVES ME

# 8. MY FAITH LOOKS UP TO THEE

# 9. JUST AS I AM

# 10. CROWN HIM WITH MANY CROWNS

# 11. COME, THOU ALMIGHTY KING

# 12. OH, WON'T YOU SIT DOWN?

# 13. O FOR A THOUSAND TONGUES

# 14. CHILDREN OF THE HEAVENLY FATHER

# 15. THE CHURCH'S ONE FOUNDATION

# 16. NEARER MY GOD TO THEE

0868.03 CMP • Flute/Oboe

# 17. PRAISE TO THE LORD, THE ALMIGHTY

# 18. ALL GLORY, LAUD AND HONOR

# 19. ALL HAIL THE POWER

# 20. GOD OF GRACE AND GOD OF GLORY

# 21. SWING LOW, SWEET CHARIOT

# 22. HE'S GOT THE WHOLE WORLD IN HIS HANDS

Swing ( ♩ = 124 )

# 23. GO TELL IT ON THE MOUNTAIN

# 24. THIS TRAIN

# 25. WHAT A FRIEND WE HAVE IN JESUS

# 26. ONWARD CHRISTIAN SOLDIERS

# 27. IN THE SWEET BY AND BY

# 28. LET US BREAK BREAD TOGETHER

# 29. CHRIST THE LORD IS RISEN TODAY

# 30. WERE YOU THERE?

# 31. THIS IS MY FATHER'S WORLD

# 32. SOFTLY AND TENDERLY JESUS IS CALLING